Flirting Tips for Guys

How to Charm, Conquer and Seduce the Woman of Your Dreams

Kevin Love

PUBLISHED BY:
Kevin Love

TABLE OF CONTENTS

Chapter 1: Getting to Grips with the Flirting Basics

Secrets on How to Flirt

The art of flirting is all about letting a person you fancy know that you are interested in her, without saying it openly. When done right, it is a choreographed dance where each person lets the other one know just how interested he is in getting to know the other, under the safety of it all being a game. If one person is interested but the other one is not, nobody is hurt because there never was a real proposition; it was all just a game. Flirting is a playground where a man and a woman can express their desire to pursue the acquaintance in hopes that it develops into a relationship or back down and leave things as they are.

Flirting is a ritual based on communication, above all. But communication can take many forms, and flirting is, believe it or not, mostly a non-verbal form of communication. Most men get nervous when it comes to talking to a woman they have just met, they don't know what to say to her. But the funny thing is, you could spend a whole night flirting with a woman without ever having to say a word to her. Ninety percent of human communication is body language and the same applies for flirting. The most vital means with which to flirt are your eyes, and they are the ones that will always tell you whether a flirt is serious or just a game.

The most fundamental thing to do when flirting with a woman is to make eye contact. More than words, more than actions, eye contact is what lets the other person know you are interested in her. When talking to another person, people spend about 20% of their time looking at the other's eyes, but this rate goes up to 40 or 50 when we have a physical or sexual interest in that person. When you are having a conversation with someone, it is somehow easier to maintain eye contact, but when there is no talking going on people tend to avoid each other's eyes, especially when you are strangers sitting in opposite sides of a room. This is what makes flirting so much more special than a regular conversation: when you flirt with somebody, you try to look at them as much as possible, even when they are not talking to you. This can be awkward at moments, but the strength with which you gaze at someone is what lets them know that you are interested in them. Looking away shyly, though not recommended, is also another way of putting your message across.

When you're standing far away from a woman that you want to flirt with, keep your eyes on her until she notices you, then slowly look away as she returns the look. Repeat this over and over, holding your gaze increasingly longer each time, until it feels comfortable just looking into her eyes. This takes practice, of course, since the first time you do it you could feel awkward and you may have lack of confidence, you will struggle to look away. All perfectly natural, but keep at it, keep looking at her with time you will feel better and it will come easier and more natural. If you are not capable of holding a woman's stare for long, you can at least let her know that you are interested by glancing back immediately after you look away. Make her know that, among all the other women present, your attention is set on her above all others. Smiling is also recommended, since it is the universal gesture of friendliness, when you are smiling you are letting people know that you have a good mood and will be nice. There are different types of smiles, however, so make sure you know what you want to convey when you do. A friendly, cheerful smile might be good if what you are looking for is a longer and more serious relationship; but if you are just looking for a one-night stand, then aim for a more sarcastic, evil-in-disguise smile. Smiling is a good way to break the ice before you start a conversation.

Eye contact is the ultimate medium of flirting since it allows you to flirt from a distance or from up close, whether the woman is alone or with friends or even a boyfriend, at a rock concert or a funeral. It is the one thing you need to work on and get comfortable with in order to flirt successfully. Some men are shy and have difficulties keeping eye contact for long; if you are one of those guys then do not worry, all you need to do is practice and your confidence will improve over time, besides all you need is a few seconds to catch someone's stare .

Laughter is the second biggest medium for flirting. Basically it boils down to making the woman you are interested in, laugh or letting her see that she makes you laugh. The second one is easier since you can just pretend everything she says is hilarious, though be careful here; you need not overdo it in case she catches on and starts thinking that you are a creep who laughs uncontrollably at anything and everything she says. The first one, making your prey laugh, is the tricky one, though it comes natural to some men. Your goal when flirting with a woman is to find out what sense of humor she has and aim for jokes based on that. If she has a sarcastic tone, or she loves silly knock-knock jokes, or some good old fashioned slapstick humor, find it out and exploit it. On the other hand, you might find that you are just mumbling incoherent phrases and yet the girl is cracking up all the time. This is your chance, it means she is flirting with you and wants to let you know, it doesn't matter what you say, you have her. Laughter releases pheromones that make us feel happy and excited, and that feeling becomes associated to the person you are with. If you are able to make a girl laugh, she will associate the feelings of happiness and excitement with being around you. Now isn't that a grand thing?

Conversation is of course important when flirting, and the good news is that it is not as difficult as most people think. Some women like to talk all the time, and if you go after one of these, all you have to do is show interest in everything she says, and you will have her eating out of your hand in no time. The most important thing is to keep your eyes on her at all times, because when she is talking of course you should be focused on her, not on anybody else. But you shouldn't just sit there and look at her, asking the right questions is a good way of verbally showing that you are following her thoughts and understand what she is talking about. One thing to note is that when you are flirting, it is a good idea to stay away from controversial topics such as politics or religion. You are trying to make her feel comfortable and relaxed around you, politics more often than not bring tension into the conversation, and the last thing you want to do is to lecture her on the political views that are up to date or correct. If you see the conversation heading towards a subject that calls for disagreement, try to steer the conversation away from it as early as possible.

Another successful way of getting noticed by women is making them feel contented and admired around you. One easy way of doing this is flattering them with compliments. While most men are not generally wired to receive compliments, women spend a lot of time thinking about how others see them, and on average, it takes them more time than men to work on their image and self-esteem. The easiest way to get on their good side is to pay them a sincere yet unique compliment. While simply telling a woman that she looks good might work, some women might brush it off as simply something you say to be nice. It is a generic comment that anybody could say, and somebody probably already has before. If, however, you notice something special about her, something that is elusive or hard to notice at first, you will score some important points. If you see a woman with an elaborate hairstyle who has obviously spent a long time working on it, complimenting her hair shows that you actually *are* paying attention to her, instead of just saying something that could apply to every other woman in the room. Aside from complimenting a woman's looks or body, it could also prove beneficial to compliment her personality or intelligence, since a lot of women find more pride in these aspects of themselves.

One really effective and fun way of flirting is by touching the girl's body in very subtle ways, or with any excuse you can think of, to get her inner desire worked up. Teaching a girl how to swing a golf club or baseball bat are great ways of doing this because in order to do so you have to put your arms around her and almost hug her all the way, though by now every girl is aware that what you are doing is just an excuse to get close to her. Still, there are less popular and less obvious ways of touching a girl. When you are handing a girl a drink at a bar, make sure your hand is covering as much of the glass as possible, so that when she grabs it she has no choice but to touch your hand. Now is the time to apply the techniques we have discussed earlier; as she is taking the drink from your hand and her fingers touch yours look her deep in the eye and smile. If what you want to do is flirt with the cute bartender, make sure to lightly graze her fingers as you hand her the cash or ATM card when you pay for a drink. After you have made your first contact, you can touch the girl on her arms using any chance you get, you can graze her hair or place a stray strand behind her ear, but if you want to touch her legs you should know that you can do it only if you are confident that you will not get slapped for doing so. You can always offer a quick massage to rub her shoulders if you see her tense or if she complains about back pain.

Always when you are flirting, it is important that you try to remain calm and relaxed so that you can be yourself; women can sense when a man is trying too hard or acting in an unnatural way, and they are usually put off by it. You should know yourself well enough to figure out which situations help you relax, and try to flirt with girls in those situations. If clubbing and bar-hopping is not your thing, it would be advisable to find ways to get comfortable in there since that is the place where you will find the most girls. In such an atmosphere, where people are drinking, everybody tends to be more relaxed and laid-back. In fact, alcohol is a great help when flirting or talking to a girl. We are not saying that you should get drunk or try to get some girl drunk. What we are trying to say is that drinking some alcohol puts everybody (or almost everybody) in a friendlier, more conversational and playful mood. Alcohol has a way of unloosening everybody's inhibitions, which is exactly what you need. Besides this relaxing effect, drinking has other effects that can help you flirt. Offering to buy a girl a drink is a great way to start a conversation, and any girl will spend at least five minutes talking to a guy that has bought her a drink.

Body language is a fundamental part of communication, and although you should be paying attention to everything the other person says, you should pay even closer attention to the way her body behaves. Her body will be much more revealing of her true intentions and desires than her actual words. First of all, if a girl is truly interested in you, her whole body and head will be oriented towards you. If she's talking to you but her entire body seems to be oriented away from you then she's just wasting your time until she finds something better. This could be your cue to change the topic of conversation to something more interesting, or you will completely lose her. The hands are another important source of clues as to what she's thinking. If she keeps fidgeting and playing around with her hands then she's probably nervous about something: it could be that you make her feel uncomfortable with the way you are behaving, or maybe she's just insecure with men. Try to find a way to calm her down, reassure her by saying something that will increase her confidence. If she keeps touching her face (especially her nose, mouth or forehead) as she talks to you, it probably means that she is lying through her teeth, so be careful what you believe. There's always a bit of lying whenever people flirt, but do not allow yourself to be fooled that easily. If her hands are always playing with her hair, however, then you are in good luck. When a woman plays with her hair, maybe twirling some strands around her finger or running her fingers through her hair, it is an almost certain sign that she is physically interested in the guy in front of her. Playing with her hair is one thing almost every woman unconsciously does when she wants to be seductive with a guy. The arms also reveal a general open or closed disposition. If her arms are open and loose, then she is receptive to whatever you are telling her. But if she holds her arms crossed across her chest in a rigid posture, you might as well give it up since it means that she's not buying any of the crap you are telling her.

Having a friend come along with you when you are trying to flirt with a girl is a good idea, since your friend could provide the support needed to make things easier. You might get nervous about talking to the girl you are into, but in that case your friend would be able to help you carry on the conversation. It would also make you feel less pressured since all the girl's attention will not be set on you but rather spread out between you and your friend. Just be careful that the girl doesn't end up liking your friend more than you! And if the flirting goes completely wrong and the girl walks off, at least you are not left standing by yourself looking like a fool.

These techniques require time to be practiced and honed down; you can't expect to become a master flirter overnight. Just remember that the ultimate goal is to have fun while meeting girls, not torture yourself over having lost a girl you met at the bar. Don't be afraid to look like a fool at times – we have all made mistakes and said the most awkward of things – but rather embrace it, laugh at yourself, shrug it off and then jump right back in the game.

Tips for Flirting with Nice Girls

There are several ways of flirting with women, which can go from very innocent and lighthearted flirting to more serious and even heavily erotic, sexual and passionate flirting. Most men can go from one range of the spectrum to the other without batting an eye, because for us it is just flirting, after all. But women are so different one from another, you can find some that will happily jump into the deep waters in the flirting game while some others are a lot more conservative and they tend to take things more seriously, which could lead to them being seriously offended by some distasteful remark you might have made simply in the spirit of flirting. Take is slow and find out who are you dealing with, just so you get no surprises.

It is recommended that, when initiating flirting with a girl you don't know, you start with the most innocent and naive flirting, and then little by little start taking it up a notch watching her reaction. If she takes it well and allows you, then continue getting into heavier flirting, but stop at the first signal that she finds your actions or comments a bit too much. There are women who are into sexual jokes and puns and this is a great way to flirt, but others are easily offended and might instantly cross you off their list because you crossed the line between flirting and being disrespectful.

There is nothing to be worried about, though, because there are plenty of fun ways to flirt with these girls without getting their backs turned at you. The first thing you should keep in mind, though, is that thing will go slower than usual, just because nice girls are not so quick to jump into bed or into a relationship with someone they just met. It will take you longer, but the rewards are well worth the wait.

What you will have to do is concentrate on making lots of eye contact, smiling at them and talking to them – that is to say, listening to them most of the time. When dealing with one of the nice girls, your priority should be to show her that you are a nice guy as well. What you should try to do is to get her to think that you are not interested in flirting just for the fun of flirting, or just to get a girl, but rather you are genuinely interested in her as a person and would like to get to know her better. Any way you have of showing that you are interested not so much in her looks but in her personality will be welcome. When complimenting her, be sure to compliment her looks, of course, but don't make it the focus of your attention. Surprise her by showing her that you remember what she had told you before; men tend to pretend that they are listening while they are thinking about something else. Finding out that a guy actually is listening to what a girl is saying immediately sends a message that he is genuinely interested.

A good first date with a nice girl is a place where you can have a long conversation. Try to avoid loud bars and discos, concerts or sporting events: the main reason you are going out with her is to learn more about her personality and so you should have the right atmosphere for doing that. If you choose to go to the movies, you will of course not be talking through the projection, so make sure to have some time after the movie to sit down for a cup of coffee and have a nice, long conversation. You even have the topic already laid out for you ("So, what did you think of the movie? What did you like and dislike about it?"). Be sure not to have any strong confrontations of opinions at first, or you could sour her. If she finds the movie fabulous – even though it was just another clichéd Hollywood romantic comedy to you – then don't tell her you hated it. Say you enjoyed it, though there were some things that you think were not great. You don't have to lie about your opinions (remember that lies are always found out in the end) but rather tone them down a bit so that you don't scare her away on the first date.

Don't be afraid to act a bit clichéd with nice girls, they like it and even expect it. While it is true that bringing her flowers may seem corny and all men feel awkward about doing it, but it will score you some big points with a typical nice girl. Also all the other small things that make up an old fashioned charming gentlemen like holding the door for her, taking her coat and helping her with the chair as she sits down are also things to remember. Once again, your goal is to play the part of the perfect gentleman firstly to gain her trust, and also to show her that you are interested in her as a person.

Sometimes trying to make a girl jealous by flirting with another girl is a good idea, and when done correctly can be lots of fun. However, when you are interested in a nice girl you should be aware that any behavior of that sort will not be tolerated. This type of girl expects your undivided attention, so you should be very careful about having a wandering eye or about smiling at another girl. Whenever you are talking about your past make sure to try as much as possible to avoid any mention about your previous relationships; in fact, if she doesn't specifically ask you about it is better to not bring them up at all. If you have many female friends, it would also be a good idea to leave them out of the conversation and just talk about the things you do with your male friends.

One thing girls like to ask is if you believe that men and women can be friends. The answer to this question is what determines what kind of guy you are, and also what kind of girl you are looking for. If you answer yes, then you are indicating that you value friendship more than any type of sexual or physical relationship, and that feelings are more important than physical attraction. If you answer the opposite, you will be showing that the most important (though of course not the only one) relationship between men and women is sexual. Don't expect to win the appreciation of a nice girl if you answer the latter.

Ways to Add More Joy and Flavor to Flirting

There is one sure way of getting frustrated and bored with flirting, and that is by doing it only thinking of the result you expect to get (be it an one-night stand or a long-term relationship). This will be frustrating because most flirting will certainly end in nothing, so you will feel like you have been wasting your time and patience with that girl only to go home empty-handed. Flirting should be approached as a game, a fun recreational activity that you do only for the fun of doing it, without expecting anything out of it. If then at the end of the night, all the flirting pays off and you end up going home with a girl, all the better. But flirting should be done because you enjoy every minute of it, because every glance at a girl, every smile and thinly-veiled innuendo is thrilling and exciting. When a girl walks out of the bar with another man in her arm leaving you all alone (and it will happen, as it has happened to all of us) you will curse yourself if your only thought was getting that girl. But you will smile to yourself and say "Oh well, better luck next time. At least I had fun for a while!" if you have the right approach to flirting.

Another idea that is good to keep in mind is that nothing is too embarrassing to be done. When flirting with a girl, you will be forced to do things you had never done before, all in order to impress the girl you set your eyes on. Singing karaoke at the top of your lungs in front of a room full of strangers, dancing tango without having any idea of what your feet are doing, going to an underground modern dance performance. In order to feel brave enough to do all this, you will have to shed all your self-consciousness aside and just jump into all sorts of crazy things. Having the ability to laugh at yourself while doing these things will be great, not only because women like a man with a sense of humor who can laugh at himself, but it will be good for you as well.

One really fun thing to do when just meeting someone at a bar, when you know you will never see that person again, is to introduce yourself as a completely different person. Change your name, your job, your hobbies and your past. Come up with another completely different story to tell and just have fun pretending to be an airline pilot on a break or a truck driver looking for some fun. Nothing constrains you to the stories you can come up with, since you know you will never see this person again. This is a great opportunity to live your childhood fantasy of being a fireman or policeman and seeing other people react to your story. As long as you have an idea of what you are talking about and don't make exaggerated claims, the other person will completely believe your story, if you tell it with enough confidence.

Going out with friends to pick up girls at the bar is a sure way to have lots of fun, while avoiding the insecurity we all normally feel when approaching a girl by ourselves. When you are out drinking and hanging out with friends, you are surrounded by people who know you and who you feel comfortable around, so putting on your charming attitude should be easier. You don't have to worry about sitting at the bar all by yourself since your friends are there; if a woman decides to walk out on you just turn around and keep talking to your friends as if nothing had happened. Holding a contest between friends to see who can get a girl's number or who gets the girl to buy them a drink first is not only fun, but also could lead to getting some sex that night (either with the girl or with your friends).

If you already have a girlfriend or wife, you can still have a lot of fun flirting. Go to a bar and sit at opposite ends, then pretend not to know each other and little by little start hitting on each other, flirting and yeah. This will be fun not only because strangers will look at you too and be amazed at the chemistry between you two, and at how fast you can pick up a girl, but also because it will allow you and your girlfriend to step out of the normal routine and try something different for the two of you. It will allow you to re-enact the passion and fire you had at the beginning and give you back those feelings of butterflies in the stomach that you may have lost since you started going steady. It's also a fun way to explore each other's fantasies and see what you can do to make them come true. You will get the best of both worlds, because you will not be wondering what the girl thinks of you or getting nervous because you might have said the wrong thing, yet you will be able to have some fun putting into practice all your smooth-talking skills.

Finally, the last thing you could try out is to go out on a double-date with friends and try to flirt with each other's girl, without taking it seriously of course. It will feel like a competition because you would be trying to take your friend's girl and he will be trying to take yours, but it's just another way of having fun. If the girls get into it as well, then all your inhibitions will be forgotten and you'll be able to enjoy a night of flirting with another girl right in front of your partner.

How Far Should Flirting Go?

Flirting is meant to be a fun activity for all people involved in it to enjoy, and the only limits to it are the ones imposed by these same people. Flirting can be done just for the fun of flirting for a while with a stranger in a bar – with no hopes or expectations of anything else happening – or it can be done in the hopes of winning the heart and eventually marrying the beautiful woman that lives next door. Just how far you take it is a personal choice. It should be clear that just because a woman flirts back at you does not mean she is actually interested in you in any way, and it could happen to you that you spend all night chatting with a girl, buying her drinks and making her laugh, only to walk back home empty-handed. These are the risks one takes, so you should know beforehand that nothing is guaranteed.

You should know that there are many motivations behind a woman's flirting, which is what makes them different from men. Men will flirt 99 percent of the time with the only goal of having sex with a woman, whether that be in the form of a one-night stand or a serious and committed relationship. Women, on the other hand, have many reasons for flirting, most of them not directly related to having sex. This is why a lot of times there are basic misunderstandings between men and women: after having spent the whole night flirting with a guy, the woman joins her friends and leaves the disco while the man is left behind wondering what he did wrong. We will try to explain what motivates women to act in such a fashion.

One of the reasons women will flirt is just because it is fun for them. They enjoy getting a man's undivided attention, having him buy her drinks, tell her jokes and entertain her, or listen to her talk for hours on end. These are the women that flirt for the sole reason of flirting, it is simply something they do to amuse themselves and have a good time. While the guy flirting with her is probably thinking "I think I'm going to get to take her home tonight!" the woman is usually just thinking "This is so much fun, I could do this all night!" The woman that does this is usually not aware that the guy is being so nice to her because he wants something from her at the end of the night. When she finally gets up and leaves at the end of the night, leaving the guy baffled, she will have no idea why the guy is upset about it. Again, it is totally acceptable for the woman to behave like this and guys should not expect anything more. These are the risks of flirting, and you should be aware of them before you start playing.

Another reason why women flirt is to raise their self-esteem. Engaging in some playful, innocent flirt with a hot guy is something that makes them feel desired, wanted and important. Women engaged in this type of flirting will especially try to get as many compliments from a guy as possible, usually related to the area they most hate about themselves: a woman with weight problems will try to get a guy to compliment her figure, while a woman who feels insecure about not being smart enough will try to have the man notice just how intelligent she is. When men realize what the women are doing they might feel used, but it shouldn't be this way.

Then there are, of course, the women that flirt because they are actually interested in the men flirting back at them. But even here the situation is not optimal, since women tend to be a lot pickier than men and they are prone to changing their idea about a man at any moment. It is quite common for a man and a woman to be flirting with each other all night long, until the man says or does the slightest thing – a vulgar joke or an ignorant comment - that makes the woman completely change her opinion about the man. In this case, again, the man will go back home empty-handed even though he was successfully flirting with the woman all night long – until he made a mistake, that is.

As it can be seen, there are many reasons why flirting with a woman might lead to nothing, even though one is doing all the right moves. We simply have to accept that flirting does not have the same meaning for men as it does for women, and therefore it is unreasonable to expect that flirting will always end up the way we want it to. What we have to keep in mind is that, along with the times we will feel like we were just wasting our time flirting with the wrong girl, there will be times when flirting will pay off. It is simply a matter of perseverance. Maybe it would be a good thing if men could also start enjoying flirting just for the fun of flirting, instead of expecting to get something out of it every time. This way, even if the flirting didn't go too far, at least you enjoyed every minute of the ride.

Is Flirting Habit-Forming?

You are a shy guy who often just goes out to the disco and spends the whole night sitting at the table drinking or standing against a wall watching everybody else have the time of their lives, talking to women, laughing and then walking home with them. You wish you could do the same but there is something that is stopping you: you don't know how to go up to a girl and start talking to her, you feel you have nothing to say, and it seems like flirting comes naturally to everybody but you. So you decide to fix that and start to practice the subtle art of flirting, and eventually you master it. You lose the fear of being turned down by a girl and start getting out there, chit-chatting away and eventually scoring big points with a few girls. But what if you went overboard and now the only way you have of interacting with a girl is by flirting?

Any type of behavior or conduct, when repeated frequently enough, can turn into a habit. Flirting is no different, and if you start using the techniques described here regularly, soon they will become second nature to you and you will employ them even without noticing it. This does not mean that you will start asking girls out without realizing it, but rather that it will become easier for you to get women to notice you, instead of just blending in with the crowd. You will not have to make an effort to let a woman know you are interested in her; instead, this will just flow from you naturally.

It does not mean that you will start flirting with every woman you meet in any situation: your boss, your friend's wife, a saleswoman at the mall or your doctor. Flirting will come to you in the environments that you have practiced it in, whether be it in a bar or a disco or any other form of social gathering. A significant thing to remember is that flirting is an activity that can happen in any situation, and so you should give yourself the opportunity to engage in flirting anywhere, as long as you do it in a respectable and appropriate manner.

Overall, being flirty all the time is not a bad thing, since you don't always have to flirt with the goal of getting a girlfriend or some casual sex in mind. You could approach flirting just as another way of interacting between men and women, a friendlier and naughtier way than just being schoolmates or workmates. It will bring a lot of fun into your life and will make your experience with women a lot more enjoyable.

Even if you did realize that you have started flirting with everyone you meet and you think it is inappropriate, this situation is much better than the one you were in before: wanting to flirt with somebody and not being able to do it. Once you have acquired the skill necessary to freely and effortlessly flirt, you will only have to make a small conscious effort to stop flirting whenever you desire to. If in some situation you consider it utterly unacceptable to flirt with somebody, it will take some mental practice to go against your newly-acquired habits, but it is not impossible. All that you will need is a bit of self-control and discipline.

Chapter 2: Naughty Or Nice?

What's the Difference between Healthy Flirting and Unhealthy Flirting?

The most important thing about healthy flirting is that it should be an enjoyable activity for everyone involved. There are almost a limitless potential to things that you can do to flirt with a girl, but there is one limit that you should never cross and that is when it starts to make the other person feel bad in any way. Of course, this limit changes from person to person so there is no way to clearly define what that limit is in general. There are things that some people will enjoy and consider it only a flirt, while some other people could be greatly offended by that very same thing. You should always pay attention to the way you're flirting makes the woman in question react, because it is not always the case that she will openly ask you to stop it because you are making her feel uncomfortable.

Flirting is a communicative act between two people and is meant to be enjoyed by both of them. The first rule of flirting is that it should never cross the border where one of the people involved feel uncomfortable, threatened or abused. What is just a silly joke to one girl could be a serious offense to another one, even though both times you just meant it as a flirt. The line between one and the other is sometimes subtle and hard to see, so when interacting with people you don't know it is advisable to take it slow at first, and if you see your actions are invited, continue doing so, but if you find any signs of resistance or avoidance on the part of the woman, then cease before you hurt or insult the other person.

On the other hand, just because you flirt with somebody doesn't mean you are actually interested in having something more significant with them. Flirting does not mean that you will end up having either a relationship or casual sex with that person. For some people, flirting is just a fun thing to do with people of the opposite sex and has no more meaning than telling a joke in front of your friends. Some treat it as a sport, challenging themselves to get somebody's attention just for the fun of it. If you are flirting with a woman hoping that you will get something from her if she flirts back, then you need to reconsider your thoughts.

Kissing can be seen as another way of flirting, especially nowadays. Some women will kiss a stranger after minutes of having met them, though this kiss should not be taken as a sign of anything more serious than just a kiss, and if she is disappointed or not completely satisfied with what she receives, she might just end the flirting after that kiss. It should not be taken as the initiation of a sexual activity, since kissing has been considered these days as rather 'harmless behavior'. Any activity involving genitals, however, is considered as unhealthy flirting or something that has utterly crossed the line of healthy flirting, and as such should not be taken lightly. It is not acceptable to touch a woman's genitals as part of flirting, and if you do so, you run the risk of being accused of molesting or severely crossing the line. Especially at work, where inevitably a lot of flirting occurs, most light flirting is acceptable but the line is drawn here. Where genitals are involved, explicit consent must be garnered or charges of sexual harassment could be pressed. We recommend men to be very careful when doing something like slapping on the ass.

You have to be very careful to respect the other person's limits and stop flirting when you get any signals that they are not into it. Otherwise, you risk crossing the border into harassment or you will be labeled as a creep and a douchebag. Always be respectful of the other person, no matter how much you might be into a girl, if she is not into you then the polite and appropriate thing to do is to stop trying to flirt with her, because she deserves some space.

Communication is essential, but remember it is a two way process so always look for the signs: is the girl enjoying herself, does she like the type of action you have chosen to flirt with her, are you making her uncomfortable or maybe she is feeling embarrassed at the attention. Healthy flirting demands that you always be respectful of the feelings your actions bring about in the person that you are flirting with. Under no circumstances are you allowed hurting anybody by flirting improperly, using abusive language or crossing the line between the fun and things that could be described as physical or mental abuse, such conduct will be considered unhealthy flirting.

The Difference Between Flirting and Being Friendly

For some people there is a very clear and definite line between flirting behavior and friendly behavior: the first is what you do with people who interest you in a romantic or sexual way, whereas the second one is what you do with people whom you like but have no romantic or sexual interest in. The behavior in both situations is almost exactly the same; you look at the person in the eye, you smile, make a few jokes and tease them a little bit. The intentions behind these attitudes, however, are very different. This is the reason why sometimes there are misinterpretations between men and women, where one of the two isn't sure whether the behavior of the other person is actual flirting or just a way of being nice.

One clear example of this is the way woman behave with gay men. A lot of women enjoy having gay friends for many reasons, one of them being that they can give themselves the chance to flirt with a guy without there being any real sexual goal. If you have ever watched a woman around a gay man, you will have noticed that they are flirting all the time in a very obvious and direct manner, but of course they both know nothing will ever happen between them. The reason is that the lack of sexual tension between them gives all the freedom to flirt away all they want, only for the pleasure of flirting. This is what we would call a friendly flirt, and it is something that men really have a hard time understanding because for them the only point of flirting is getting the sexual release. Relationships between two straight men or two straight women, however, are never flirty at all, because there is no room for it. Even though the behavior might at times look surprisingly similar, to that of a couple of strangers flirting, there is no sexual motivation for it so no.

For other people there is no difference at all between flirting and being friendly, there is just a difference between the way you behave around men and the way you behave around women. That is to say, flirting is something you do with every woman, not just the ones you are specifically interested in. If you are lucky and one of the women you are flirting with happens to respond, then you can consider engaging in more serious flirting.

For these men, flirting is more related to being a gentleman around woman and is not specifically tied to being interested in them. Opening a door for them, holding their coats for them, helping them with the chair when they take a seat, being polite and courteous all the times are part of the natural way men should behave towards women, just because of the fact that they are women. Failing to behave in such a manner would be considered rude and impolite.

One thing that could set them apart is that while flirting you are always somehow trying to trick or deceive the other person, show her the best side of you or put on a show that might contradicts the way you really are. When flirting, your goal is to impress charm and woo the girl in front of you, and sometimes the truth can be left far behind in order to achieve that. With friends, however, it is much easier to open up and let our true selves come out. We have nothing to hide from them and showing our best side is not a priority. We are not saying that there is no room for honesty in a romantic relationship, what we are saying is that honesty comes later on, after we have managed to portray the best first impression and not at the flirting stage.

To flirt you do basically anything that will get you the attention of a girl and will let her know that you have some interest in her and that you want to get to know her better. That means that you will want to come across as attractive and interesting and it will involve effort on your part to give a good impression. When you are just being nice, however, you do not have to worry so much about the impression you are making on the people you communicate with. You can be nice basically with anyone you interact with, but when you are flirting with a specific goal you will pick the target more carefully.

What's the Difference Between Play Flirting and Real Flirting?

Flirting is part of our everyday life. Many people flirt as part of their everyday interaction with their colleagues of the opposite sex at work or with their friends in their free time. Some people flirt all of the time while other flirt less, but everyone does it at some point even unconsciously. Noticing your friend's new hairstyle and complimenting it, or smiling at another while helping her pick something she had dropped or making a fun joke at the bar. At the office you may flirt with your boss's secretary just to get that signature you need from him. Everyone does that, and that kind of behavior is part of friendly relationships. When it is a spontaneous thing that you do just to feel good around women and also to make them feel good around you it will be considered play flirting. Most guys who flirt a lot will be considered nice and fun to spend time around and therefore will become popular among their friends. Having a good time is the main goal of flirting, but even when you will be looking for a relationship it will only make it easier for you making you look more appealing to potential girls. You will find it easier to interact with them and you will be more confident when asking them out.

Play flirting may become so natural to you that you will not notice it when you do it, but people around you will notice, especially girls. However, you will notice how the girls react to your flirting and it will be obvious to you when a girl will be interested in you, if you feel the same way about that girl you are at a great starting position to begin your game. That is when the flirting will seriously start and the manner of your actions will change from play flirting to something more serious and more aggressive. At this point, you want your flirting to get the right signals across to the girl. You may try to find ways to see her under any little pretexts spending as much time around her as you can. When you are sure that she is up for the game, you can start getting even closer to her, you can complement her perfume or touch her hair when you are talking to her. Adjust your pace of actions to whatever the girl will allows and do not forget to always keep the flirting game polite and fun without pushing too fast and too hard. A guy that wants to always be in control and is also demanding will pass as someone who is pushy and rude. Take your time and do not rush things. While you are still flirting, you are at the same time making her aware as to the nature of your interest in her, touching her will leave no doubts about your intentions. Serious flirting is definitely more aggressive but at the same time should still be a fun and joyful way to reach your goal which is asking the girl out to a date.

While in play flirting, you are just having a good time and entertaining your female friends. In real flirting, the point is to let the other person knows of your romantic intentions where the flirting may be more physical and direct. In any case, your goal in real flirting is to get the girl to go out with you, after that you may even want to continue a relationship.

The Lines between Innocent Flirting and Dangerous Flirting

Anything that can be considered healthy flirting or play flirting will be innocent at the same time. Whenever you just flirt for fun and keep your actions within the comfort zone of the people involved, you need not worry if you are treading into a danger zone. When however, you are interested in a woman romantically you will want to start flirting seriously and going further with your actions, and this is when you need to be careful and consider if the woman likes what you are doing. Remember flirting is like a dance you make a move and your partner reacts to it following your lead, if she does not follow then there is no dancing. Always pay attention to the reactions and you will know if you can go further. If you came as far as touching her body than you may want to keep an eye for any signs that she feels uncomfortable. Sometimes she may not say it out loud, she may be embarrassed and it will be enough for her to not enjoy your actions.

Likewise if you are planning to do anything that goes beyond touching the acceptable parts of the female body and you should seek consent from the woman in question. The acceptable parts are those that you could touch in public without making anyone embarrassed. Here there is no doubt that you are getting too close to making the game dangerous. If you try to get too far the woman may feel abused and this is not just about her comfort zone, flirting was supposed to be fun so if she is not enjoying and is not ready to go any further ,you have to immediately stop. Never put a woman in such a position where she could feel endangered or that she has no control over the situation and is being pushed to doing something she does not want to.

There can be another danger at play. That is when you are flirting with a woman unsuspecting that she has a jealous man. You are the one who is going to be in the uncomfortable position in this case. You may also fall into the trap of simply making a bad choice of the woman that you are flirting with if she is for instance underage, you could get yourself into problems with the legal authorities. Some women may press charges if they felt harassed by your actions. We encourage playing it on the safe side making sure that the woman is simply into the game and does not feel pushed in any way.

Chapter 3: Getting Noticed! Making Contact

The Best Way to Ask A Girl Out on a Flirt Date

The playing ground for dating is heavily unbalanced between men and women. Women are constantly showered with offers and propositions; men are constantly approaching them trying to get their attention. They will grant us men sometimes a few minutes, sometimes seconds, maybe not even that, to convince them of why they should grant us a date with them. This is why it is up to us men to come up with ways of impressing them and making ourselves stand out from the crowd. Every woman is asking herself "Why should I go out with this guy?" and it is up to us to give her an answer.

An essential thing you need to know before you attempt to ask a girl out is what your strengths are. Are you the guy that can always make a woman laugh? Are you the intellectual type, who charms women with his vast knowledge on any and every subject? Are you the handsome guy with the perfect body? Knowing what you are good at will allow you to choose your plan of action better. Knowing yourself will also let you know early on whether you have any chances or not with a woman, before you decide to invest your time on her. Going after a girl who you know has a history of going out with jocks and bodybuilder-types when you are a tiny, scrawny nerd is sure to be a waste of time and lead to nothing but frustration.

The second thing you need to know, and very much related to the previous point, is to know something about the girl you intend to ask out. If she is a friend, classmate or workmate then this shouldn't be so difficult, since you'll have plenty of opportunities to scope her out. If, however, you want to ask out a girl you just met at the disco, it is a bit trickier to do a background check. You will have to rely mostly on your gut feeling, but there are some things you can do to maximize your chances. The basic rule is to observe your target and try to get as much information as possible. Watch her interact both with her friends and other men who approach her. Does she prefer light conversation or deep and emotional exchanges? Do you see her laughing out loud all the time and jumping from conversation to conversation or is she focused and listening attentively to one person? If the former, then it means she is in the mood for some light fun; try to approach her with some funny anecdote, try to make her laugh at any cost. If however, she is the latter, then maybe she is more into an actual, meaningful conversation. You could choose from any topic that comes to mind, as long as you feel comfortable talking about it.

When proposing an activity for your date, there are two main strategies you could pick from. They are, respectively, to cater to your taste or to cater to hers. Each has its own advantages and disadvantages, as is to be expected. Proposing an activity that you like and are interested is a good idea because it is something you will feel comfortable with, and it will allow you to be relaxed and calm on your first date, letting you focus on impressing and charming the lady. You will, ideally, choose an activity that excites you and motivates you, and you will therefore be able to transmit and share that excitement and motivation to your date. You will show yourself at your best, doing something you enjoy and at which you have some level of expertise. This will give you the chance to impress your date with your abilities and skills. The disadvantage, on the other hand, is that you run the risk of having the girl not interested at all in the idea you proposed. If you fail to communicate your enthusiasm then you will have the girl bored out of her mind for the entire date, which is obviously not the best scenario. The second option, catering to the girl in question's preferences, has the obvious benefit of ensuring that the girl will be happy doing something she enjoys. If it just happens to be something you hate, then you'll have to suck it up and put up with it. Remember that you are there to get the girl, not to spend a night playing your favorite video game. Just keep your mind on the goal, smile all the way through and think that a night of knitting with the volunteers at the elder's home will score you some big points with the girl you want. The down side to this is that, since you might be doing something you are not familiar with; you might tense up, get nervous or feel like you have to prove yourself in front of this girl, which of course will not set the greatest atmosphere. One of the most fundamental things to keep in mind is that the activity chosen is secondary, or even simply an excuse. The only reason you are there is to get to know this girl and show her just what a great guy you are.

The one indisputable benefit about proposing an activity yourself is that it makes you look like a guy who is comfortable taking the lead, being in charge. This is something that most women find definitely attractive. The best possible scenario is the one where you are smart enough to find out exactly what activity she's interested in – without asking her explicitly – and then proposing simply this. This will gain you the double advantage of catering to her taste while still making you look like you were taking the lead. It will also make you come off as a sensitive guy who is capable of choosing an activity that perfectly suits the taste of the girl.

One thing you have to consider before asking the girl out is whether you will ask her out on a real date or whether you will try to spend some time with her without acknowledging that you are actually out on one. Some women might say they are not dating at the moment, or they have boyfriends or any other imaginable reason why they don't want to date. You can always bypass this objection by saying that you are not asking her on a date, you just want her help picking out a present for your family at the mall; or that you need to go to the museum for a class assignment and you would like her to accompany you, since her knowledge of art is superior to yours.

Tips on How to Approach a Stranger that Has Caught Your Interest

We have all been there. You see an incredibly gorgeous woman on the street or in a cafe and you are dying to go up to her and start talking to her, but you have no idea how to open up a conversation. You do not want to look like a creep who talks to just anybody on the street, but if you do not act soon the girl of your dreams might walk away any minute. The one thing you should keep in mind when approaching a stranger is that you do not want to seem desperate to make contact. You should, above all, remain calm and cool; not indifferent and apathetic but not overly enthusiastic. It is important to remember that whoever you are approaching is not the last woman you will meet in your life; if things do not work out with her, there will be other women to talk to and ask out. Failure is something that's always possible and we should not fear it or make it desist from attempting anything, failure is the opportunity to learn. Given this, we still want to maximize our chances for success, and here is how to do that.

An interesting way to approach somebody and start a conversation is by finding something you both have in common and exploiting it. Social events like art exhibitions, music concerts and sports and charity events are a great opportunity for this, because the simple fact that you are both present already entails you have something in common. This strategy is a bit more difficult to put to use in discos or pubs because it is not obvious what it is that you and your potential date has in common. But even the smallest things are an excuse to get close and talk to somebody. A friend of mine started a conversation that turned into an ongoing relationship with a woman on the street just because he saw her fiddling with the latest iPhone, which he had bought a week before. This apparently insignificant coincidence is what sparked the conversation and brought them together.

One thing to consider is just how honest you want to be with the things you claim to have in common with the woman you are seeking. Pretending to be interested in art just to get a date with a gorgeous lady you met at the museum is something that has worked countless times, but in the long run the truth comes up. When she realizes you know little about art and care even less, and the consequences could be worse than if you had been honest from the start. On the other hand, that white lie may give you enough time to win her over with your real personality and by the time she realizes you were just bluffing at the museum, she will no longer care cause you will have won her over with your other charms. That is if your foot does not slip right there in the museum and your ignorance come right out.

If the person you are interested in is a colleague from work, someone you see frequently in the office but never have the chance to talk to, take the time to find out what she likes to do in her free time, ask her friends and other colleagues, and then you can go up to her and engage in conversation. The office is always a fertile ground for flirting and there is always a possibility to find out some details about the person you are interested in. Even if you do not find much about her, you already work for the same company and you can always start from there. Depending on what each of you does in the company, you can always find a way to seek her help or help her out in some way.

Now we are moving on to another technique, difficult to master for some men because it implies putting themselves in a weak position. This strategy, however, has proven to work far better than the ones listed above, given that one practices a bit and doesn't overdo it. Whereas before we discussed approaching women offering something of your own (knowledge on certain topics, funny quips), now you are going up to women empty-handed and asking for their help. The idea here is to pretend ignorance, disorientation or any other disability in order to start a conversation.

Let's imagine, one more time, we see an incredibly gorgeous woman at an art gallery. This time, instead of starting a conversation based on your knowledge, let's do it based on your ignorance. Something along the lines of the following might work: "Hi, I'm not really an art buff, I just came because the exhibit sounded really interesting but I'm having problems making sense of what I'm seeing, putting it in context. What is the artist trying to say here?" And from this honest admittance of your ignorance two things could happen. The woman in question might just happen to be an art connoisseur and she'll gladly give you a tour of the place, which will makes her feel good about herself because she gets to show off her knowledge in front of a man, she gets to feel the power of holding the upper hand. In the other scenario, the woman might be in your same situation, not having much of an idea of what she's looking at. This is the perfect opportunity to offer her your company as you both try to make your way across the artistic maze you're in, deciphering the strange paintings on the walls.

When we say that this strategy should not be overdone we mean that you should not stretch your ignorance too far and pretend to be clueless about everything, depending on your new-found partner to survive. Woman like holding the upper hand, having some power and control, but they don't want to carry a defenseless baby around. Even when you are being given a master lesson on contemporary art by the woman you picked up, you should not relinquish control absolutely and say 'do with me as you will'. You could exert some power by leading the way through the gallery ('oh, that exhibit we can do later, let's go this way now') or by setting the pace ('what do you say we take a break for a few minutes and go get something to drink?'). Whatever you do, you need to show her that despite your ignorance in the field, you are capable of taking the reins and leading the night on.

One crazy idea that works out every now and then is what we call 'brutal honesty'. You have to be very careful who you choose to practice this on, since a lot of woman will be scared off by this tactic, but if you find a girl confident enough to put up with it, you will be just fine. The strategy in question consists of going up to a stranger without any excuse or story and in a very direct and straightforward manner telling her that you find her unbelievably beautiful and you would never forgive yourself passing up the opportunity to talk to her. Since this is one of the most direct methods of flirting and your intentions are out in the open, conversation can flow in a much freer way, and you can ask all the questions you want without seeming invasive. You can introduce yourself and ask for the girl's name, what she does for a living, if she's single or not and anything else you might want to know. It will be clear from the start that you are interested in asking her out or having an encounter with her, so you don't have to waste time pretending to be just trying to get to know her in a friendly way. The girl on her part will also be brutally honest and she will not keep you hanging on for a long time without really being interested in you. If you choose the wrong girl to do this with, the worst thing that could happen is that she will turn around and walk away without saying a word, or she will just tell you to leave her alone. So as you see there is nothing to lose and there is no reason why you should not try this tactic.

Ways to Turn Flirting into Something More

From the moment you start flirting, even with just a simple glance her way, you should be doing two things simultaneously: showing her you are interested, and finding out what her situation is. You may spend all night at a pub smiling back and forth with a woman just to find out at the end of the night that she was there accompanying her husband, who is sitting at the other end of the table. Needless to say, your chances of getting anything more than a flirt have been drastically reduced to zero.

There is a lot of information you should be picking up to see what your chances of anything more than the flirts are. First, finding out if she is in a relationship and just how committed to it she is. If you don't have a problem with it, not even the fact that the woman has a boyfriend or husband is reason enough to stop flirting, given that infidelity rates for women in the US are close to 50% (meaning, one out of every two women admit to having cheated while in a relationship more than once). If you are looking for a relationship instead of a one-night stand, another thing to keep an eye out for is when this person ended her last relationship. If she is just coming out of a three-year engagement, chances are she's not going to be too crazy about jumping into a new relationship right away.

After you gather some information and come to the conclusion that she might be open to something (from a one-night stand to a serious, long-term relationship and anything in between), it is time to start acting. Depending on what you want you will act differently, but the main thing is to not be afraid to get rejected. You will always be rejected by somebody; the vital thing to keep in mind is that there are plenty of other women out there to be had.

When going after a one-night stand, you only have to keep up the flirting for a couple of hours at the bar trying to charm the woman you chose, so in this case you have to be a bit aggressive: flirt constantly and in any way possible, never let her out of your sight, talk to her continuously. If you see any other men go up to her and engage her in conversation, find a way to interrupt them or get her attention, or at least join the conversation. Usually going up to her and offering her a drink you bought at the bar is a good excuse to join any conversation.

Since you are only after a one-night stand, after which you will probably never see that person again, don't be afraid to distort the truth a bit in order to impress her. Tell her about the trip you just made to the Bahamas (even though it was actually your friend who did that) or about the cool volunteering you do for some ecological organization. Don't make up outrageous lies since it will be hard to back them up, and women can be turned off when they suspect men are lying. But borrowing stories from other people or exaggerating your own stories a bit should be safe enough.

If, on the other hand, what you are looking for is more of a long-term relationship, then your approach should be different. In this case it is advisable to always tell the truth and nothing but the truth, since any lie you may use just to get the girl probably will be found out later on. The good thing is that you don't have just one night to act but probably many encounters in which to charm the beautiful lady.

In a situation when the woman you're flirting with is a colleague from work or somebody you see on a regular basis, it is advisable to take it slowly. There is no need to rush since you will be seeing this person quite often, giving you the time needed to little by little gain her trust and woo her with your dazzling personality and stunning looks. A progressive approach is recommended, starting with little, innocent flirting and slowly, day after day, increasing the intensity. You may start off just by making conversation with her, or looking her way every now and then and smiling at her. After that you might move on to some physical contact, for example by offering to rub her shoulders if she complains about back pain. Asking her if you can join her for lunch is also a great idea if you work or study together, since it is not actually considered a date and yet it affords you the opportunity to talk to her outside of the usual environment you see her in, thus creating more intimacy. Calling her on the phone after work is also a good move, of course you use some work-related excuse to start the conversation but then slowly move on to more personal matters. And it is always a good idea to end a phone call by making her laugh. That way, laughter will be the last thing she experienced with you and will associate you to that good feeling. After this flirting has been going on for a while and you feel confident and secure around her it is time to ask her out: ask her if she would like to accompany you to the movies on the weekend (by now you should know her taste in movies so you could recommend something she will like) but don't offer to take her out to dinner. The date should be seen as just friends from work getting together on a weekend, nothing more. If that first date goes well, and you feel there is some real chemistry, then it is time to go for it and ask her out to dinner (again, by now you probably know what type of food she's into) and make it your first official date.

You should remember that flirting has the three stages, each of which follows a very different set of rules. In the first stage, the approach, it is the first contact you make with the girl, where sometimes in just a matter of seconds you both decide whether you want to give each other a chance or not. The approach can be the first look you exchange, the first words you say to each other or the first moment you start dancing with a stranger. The next stage is the conquest, where both partners have implicitly agreed to play the flirting game for a bit and they now have the objective of charming each other. This is what you will spend most of your time doing, whether it be chatting to a girl or finding subtle ways of touching her as you dance together or complimenting her on her looks. This is the part where both men and women seriously evaluate whether they actually want to have something to do with the other person, and even if that is a viable option. The last stage of flirting, the wrap-up, is what you arrive to if you don't make any mistakes in the two previous stages. This is where all your hard work pays off or goes down the toilet: the moment where you ask the girl out on a date or ask her to go home with you for the night. While the two previous stages are subtle, in this one you have to put yourself out there and ask the girl out in an explicit way, to show her that you mean business and you are willing to risk being rejected.

Chapter 4: Unwanted Admirers May Strike!

Ways to Get Women to Stop Flirting with You

We have been talking about the ways to flirt with a woman, but what happens when we get an unwanted attention on their part? Women, the same as men, will only flirt when they believe their actions will be reciprocated or at least encouraged. Because of this, the easiest and most effective way to get women to stop flirting with you is to show them explicitly and emphatically that you are not interested. The way to do this is by acting the opposite of how we described in the first chapter.

The first and most obvious action is to avoid eye contact, that is, to pretend not to see the woman flirting with you at all. If you do make eye contact, however, you should try to give her a cold, distant look, showing no emotion or interest whatsoever. This technique has to be done right, however, since a mistake might actually give the wrong impression. If you avoid her eyes most of the time but then quickly look at her and look away, the girl will think you like her but are just afraid to show it. You should spend most time avoiding her eyes, and if by accident your eyes meet, don't look away quickly but rather hold her gaze for a moment, in a cold and uninterested way. Another thing to keep in mind is that you shouldn't avoid facing her direction, as in turning away or anything. If the girl is talking to you, it would be impossible to look the other way; what you do instead is focus on some object located behind her so that you are facing her but also looking her past. This will certainly get the message across that you are not interested in pursuing anything with her.

In some cases, of course, it would be considered rude or even impossible to avoid eye contact, but there are still ways of getting the message across. Again, the point is to behave in a cold and distant manner, so as to show her that you are clearly not interested in her advances. Refraining from smiling is a good way to do so, and not laughing at her joke is another one. These two, if done excessively, could make you seem rude to the other person, which is something you probably don't want. The trick is to use these techniques just the right amount, without overdoing it.

Some women can take the lead when it comes to getting compliments, and if you do not say anything nice about them they will ask you themselves, trying to get your opinion about their hair, their clothes or their shoes. Your answer should be as neutral as possible, again without being rude or offensive. Avoid directly expressing your opinion, as in "I like your hair/clothes/shoes" but rather state it as a fact unrelated to you. Something along the lines of "your hair/clothes/shoes are nice" with a neutral emotional response will usually work. Another common strategy for women are to "fish for compliments", that is, say something negative about themselves in a straightforward manner in an attempt to get you to contradict them and say something nice about them. They could say, for example, "This dress is so ugly" or "I hate the way my hair looks tonight", where the reply they are trying to get from you is "No, that dress looks really good on you" or "Your hair looks beautiful". If you notice a woman fishing for compliments, the best strategy is to politely ignore her comments and quickly change the subject of conversation. This will conveys the message that you either agree with her negative comment or are simply not interested in playing along with her.

If a woman asks you out to dance with her, it is a clear sign of flirting, especially considering that it is typically man's role to be the one who asks out to dance. In this case you should refuse to dance with her at any cost, otherwise the flirting will only escalate. Some polite ways of getting out of dancing are claiming to be embarrassed about the way you dance or being too tired to dance. This might get you labeled as a boring, lame person, but this is better than being stuck dancing with a person who thinks you are interested in her. The risk with this scenario, though, is that you might get caught dancing with another woman later in the night, putting you in a tight spot.

One erroneous strategy some men take is to talk about their wife or girlfriend in an attempt to show a woman that they are already taken. This is a big mistake since many women consider talking about relationships to be just another way to flirt. If you do not wish to lead them on, it is a good idea to mention you are already committed to another person but without spending too much time talking about it. State clearly and directly that you are in a relationship but don't discuss the details of that relationship with a woman trying to flirt with you.

Finally, the best way to get the message across that you are not interested in a woman is to be cold and distant to her and at the same time let her see you openly flirting with another woman. Simply ignoring or avoiding a woman's flirting might lead her to think that you are just playing hard to get and, therefore, she should try harder. When on the other hand you do your best to ignore her while you are simultaneously flirting with another woman, then it is a clear sign that you do not want to have anything to do with her, without coming off as rude or impolite.

Basically any way you choose to act it is up to you but the bottom line is that you have to stay polite while explicitly letting the woman knows that you are not interested in pursuing a flirt with her. Flirting is a form of communication all you need to do is never pick up the receiver.

Ways to Tell Your Friend's ExGirlfriend to Stop Flirting with You

Imagine the following scenario: your best friend, whom you've known since you were kids, starts going out with a gorgeous, intelligent and funny woman. After going out a couple of times things get serious, and they make it official: they are in a relationship. You hang out with them a lot and you start to envy your friend a bit for having found such a great woman. Some months after that, your friend tells you that he actually does not have any feelings for her and that there is just no chemistry between them. He ends the relationship, though they both swear to keep on being friends. So, you think to yourself, this is my opportunity; he dumped her so now I can go after her!

Before you do anything, we advise you to take a step back, take a deep breath and really think about what you are going to do. Dating a friend's ex-girlfriend is one of the most complicated situations you can get yourself into. No matter how much your friend says it is ok, he has no more feelings for her and you should go for it, but even if you feel like it is worth it, do not be so naive as to believe that. There will be complications, there will be feelings of jealousy and there will be fights with your friend that may end up ruining a life-long friendship. Unless you are absolutely sure that the woman in question is the one for you, the woman of your life, it is not worth losing a friend over something like this. Even in the unlikely case that your friend actually is ok with you dating his ex-girlfriend, you may not end up being ok with it in the long run. Knowing that your friend has heard your current girlfriend's most intimate secrets and confessions or has slept with her might be enough to make you start feeling begrudged towards him. Our advice is to forget about such a girl and move on to another one; as the saying goes, there's plenty of fish in the sea.

An alternate scenario, just as complicated and tricky, is the one where your friend's ex-girlfriend is the one interested in you and actually does something about it. Even if you do not do anything about it, having her flirt with you is just as likely to sour the friendship you had as if it were you the one doing the flirting. There are many ways of handling this but none of them are easy though.

Your first action in a situation like this should be to ignore her flirting all the time. Here you should use the strategies we have already covered earlier in the chapter. You should avoid eye contact with her, even to the point of appearing shy. You should listen to her when she talks to you (not doing so would be rude) but you should not encourage her by asking her a lot of questions. Always try to avoid conversations related to personal matters, and talking about her previous relationship with your friend is something you should avoid at all costs. Hopefully by simply ignoring her flirting she will get the message that you are not interested in her. If in spite of this she continues, there are more direct measures to take.

Your next move should be to confront the girl and tell her, very clearly and without beating around the bush, that you value the relationship you have with your friend too much, and you would not like to get involved with an ex-girlfriend of his. Tell her that her flirting makes you feel uncomfortable and that you feel it could jeopardize your friendship, so you would greatly appreciate it if she would stop it. If she asks you whether you have feelings for her (a lot of women might ask "if I hadn't been in a relationship with your friend, do you think something could have happened between us?") the best answer is that you never actually thought of her that way, you never felt anything for her, simply because being your friend's girlfriend automatically marked her as out of bounds. Never, under any circumstances, say that you would like to have something with her, only her past relationship prevents you from it. This will only encourage her, which is something you do not want.

If, in spite of all this she persists flirting with you, then the next thing to do is to completely avoid her for a while, until things cool down a bit.

A simple thing you might want to consider doing, while you do everything described above, is being honest with your friend and telling him about the situation you have in your hands. Be sincere and concise, letting him know that you think his ex-girlfriend is flirting with you but you are not interested in it and you are trying to ignore her flirting. Doing this will put you on the safe side, because one thing you do not want is to have the ex-girlfriend go up to your friend and tell him that you are the one flirting with her, just out of spite. It is better to think ahead and play it safe, better to prevent than to repair?

How to Get a Teacher to Stop Flirting with You?

It has been every boy's fantasy to have something with a teacher from school. We have all had a crush on our third grade teacher, and we have all had a super-hot science teacher that we could not stop looking at, no matter how boring the subject she was trying to teach. As you grow older you start to learn how to flirt with your teachers, and some young teenagers are lucky enough to have the teacher flirt back. In college, the fantasy has the chance of actually coming true, when the attraction turns into flirting and the flirting turns into a hot affair in the university corridors. All of this is great, if you happen to be interested in actually having something with the teacher. In the unlucky scenario where you want nothing to do with the teacher but she is interested in you, things are quite different.

Having an unwanted teacher flirt with you is a difficult situation to deal with because you are caught in the middle of a power -struggle- where you hold the weak position. If the flirting becomes inappropriate it could escalate to sexual harassment and in that case the sensible thing to do is to contact the school authorities. However, if the flirting behavior is too mild to merit the title of harassment, there are other things you can do to put a stop to it.

The first thing you need to know is that most teachers will not want their flirting to become a public issue, so they will avoid doing it in front of the rest of the class. Therefore, avoiding being in one-on-one situations with the teacher should limit her opportunities to flirt with you. This is the single most effective strategy, and it is also quite easy to put into practice. There will be no flirting in class, of course, because no teacher would be crazy enough to let everybody else in the classroom know they are interested in you. Since 90 percent of the time in school is spent inside the classroom, at least you know that while there you are safe. Inside the classroom you should also avoid making eye contact as much as possible, just so that the teacher doesn't get the idea that you are interested in pursuing a relationship with her. The rest of your time in school, outside of the classroom, you should spend it surrounded by friends all the time. If the teacher never sees you alone, she will have no opportunity to approach you. This doesn't mean you have to live in fear, always looking behind your back to see if the teacher is coming near you. It just means that you should minimize the time you spend alone, so as to not give the teacher a chance to get close to you.

The other principal thing you should do is keep any conversation or discussion you may have with the teacher focused exclusively on academic topics. In the case that it is unavoidable to be in a one-on-one situation with the teacher, don't let the conversation wander off into personal topics such as your interests, hobbies or friends. If the teacher starts talking about herself, don't interrupt her (that will make you come off as rude), simply let her finish and then take the conversation back to its original subject. A woman trying to flirt with you will inevitably talk about herself; she will tell you all about her daily routine and her musical tastes, what her favorite food is and where she went on her last holiday. If you ask her more questions, you will be encouraging her in her flirting and she will start to get more and more intimate in the things she tells you, starting to talk about her previous boyfriends and her family issues. At this point it will be too late for you to cut off the flirting without angering her, so it is best to prevent things from happening from the beginning.

One big mistake most people make is thinking that flirting with a teacher is a great way to get good grades without too much effort. They will openly engage their teacher in a flirting game that, while harmless and even beneficial at first, could lead to very complicated scenarios later on. What you always have to remember is that the teacher is the authority, she has the power inside the classroom, and should anything go wrong in what you thought was an innocent flirting game, you will be paying the consequences. Your grades can drastically drop, just as fast as they went up when the teacher held you in her favor. Your reputation, if word gets out that you are having some sort of affair with the teacher, could also be seriously damaged.

If the flirting or harassing continues even after you attempted to avoid the teacher, simply let her know that you are ready to go to the authorities and inform them about her behavior towards you. This should certainly let her think twice and may scare her into leaving you alone. When you talk to your teacher about this you must remain calm and serene, she has to think that you have thought this out all the way through and it is not something you just came up with to frighten her. The effect will be bigger if you are the one approaching your teacher when she is alone and telling her this, instead of letting her approach you and then using the occasion to tell her. It will put you in the predator's role going after the prey and not the prey trying to somehow defend himself from the predator. If this is not enough to put a stop to the harassing, then take the extra step and actually go to the authorities with your story. Tell them you tried to stop it in several attempts but you found yourself with no choice but to do this. Stress the fact that you are not interested in ruining the teacher's reputation; you simply want her to leave you alone.

Chapter 5: The "In-A-Relationship" Flirt

Is Flirting Considered Cheating?

There are more than one way flirting can be understood. In some cases it's just a fun thing to do, there are some people who flirt habitually all the time and with everybody, it's just the way they are. A married man can for instance flirt with his female personnel at the office, and if the flirting is kept within a good taste and the comfort zone of all the parties it can be considered a healthy and fun way of interacting. Make sure, however, that your intentions are clear so that the woman does not get it the wrong way. Of course, in an environment where people have time to get to know each other, such behavior will develop over time and become a part of the company's culture. This type of flirting will not be taken beyond the little fun it brings and therefore, it will not be considered cheating. Sharing a few jokes and laughs as well as smiles can be a fun part of any relationship and will be accepted by most people in the usual situations as a normal thing. Tip: beware of jealous boyfriends cheating or not, sending a flirting smile towards a girl might get you into trouble.

There is a thin line between a fun flirt and a serious one, and while a fun flirt is definitely innocent the serious one may sometimes be misinterpreted. When you are in a situation between people who are strangers to each other it can always be taken the wrong way. Not knowing a person's way of being may lead to an uncomfortable situation where someone may completely misunderstand your intentions, and even when your action was intended as a light flirt, you may be considered as one who instigates improper behavior. Even if flirting is just an early stage of getting acquainted with a person, some bystanders may even interpret this as a part of an intimate relationship that you are having in secret with the woman you are flirting with. This fact justifies the reason why some people might jump into conclusions that you are in fact cheating with that person. It may prove to be risky to flirt too obviously with someone you have just met, especially not knowing if they are in a relationship. You should do your homework and find out the facts before you get too far into the game, especially if you are in a business environment where the game becomes serious anyway. Of course, it always depends on the situation you are in; you may not be so concerned in a bar but if you are doing business, too much may be at stake.

Some people will not let their partners flirt fearing that it will lead to something else. As we said flirting is just a game, but the main purpose of flirting is to get you some action and this little fact may change the way people understand and approve or disapprove of your behavior. Keep this in mind when flirting and you will stay out of trouble. Additionally, flirting may become physical at some stage, and here again it depends on the circumstances, but touching a woman's body may be considered as crossing the line between a decent activity and something more serious and improperly provoking . Some people will consider physical contact as cheating even when it does not lead to actual intercourse. The line here is very vague, and we recommend staying on the safe side and avoiding anything that could be misinterpreted. On the other hand, some people would even consider a quick passing kiss on the lips as acceptable. If such kisses are part of your relationship, even with close friends you are treading on a thin ice; all too easy to cross the line at some point. That is why flirting can lead to cheating and at the same time can be seen as unwelcome. It is not the flirting that is feared but the consequences that it inevitably may lead to on so many occasions.

In some cultural contexts flirting may be a dangerous thing to do; you may want to consider the social and religious realities of the country you are living in. In some cultures flirting is not welcome or even forbidden and women who are found flirting are considered impure and unchaste even if they are not married. In those communities such activity will not be tolerated, it will be considered cheating and sometimes even prosecuted.

Flirting can border on cheating if it is meant to encourage further intimate contact. In other words, if you are flirting with the intention to get something out of it, then yes, it should be considered cheating if the girl is in a relationship. But most of the time flirting is a way of making new acquaintances as well as maintaining established relationships without having to lead to anything significant that could be considered cheating.

Is It Wrong to Flirt with Others Even If You're Completely Faithful with Your Partner?

As said before light flirting in itself is not cheating, therefore there should be nothing wrong with flirting even when you are completely faithful to your partner, or rather especially when you are. When a relationship is built upon trust, maintaining a fun and happy environment becomes natural. That can include spontaneous and fun flirting on the part of each of the partners. It feels good when guys flirt with your woman; it means that she is exceptional, and she is yours nonetheless. How exciting it is to be the one to hold the girl that everyone else would like to have? Your woman will also feel wanted and admired and it will increase her self-worth. Likewise your woman will happily look at other women flirting with you, because she will know that they cannot take you away. It's a win-win situation; both sides feel uplifted while no one gets hurt.

So if you are faithful flirt away, but, there is always a BUT because human relationships are complicated. In situations when there has been a history of mischief, even if you are the one who has cheated, you might feel less confident about your partner flirting with a stranger. Knowing from experience where it can lead, you may picture your woman in the arms of the guy flirting with her. Hence you may expect or fear that your partner will let the flirt turn into something more. In such a situation it could end up with unwanted arguments. So, if you don't have full confidence in her loyalty and can't control your temper, you would be better off addressing the situation ahead of time, gently indicating that you do not like it when she flirts. But here you may need to remember that this may alert her suspicions. After all she is a woman and they have a sixth sense as it is, you may want to avoid feeding it. On the other hand, if you know of any previous indiscretions on the part of your partner you will understandably feel threatened. Each flirtatious look from an unsuspecting guy will trigger warning signs the size of Alaska. The question is why are you still together? But since you are, it will be advisable to give her a warning, because she should know what to expect if you catch her flirting with someone.

Of course, there are relationships where flirting will always be considered unacceptable and wrong. When extreme jealousy is involved on the part of one of the partners the result can never be good. In such cases even an innocent look at a passerby may trigger a full blown rage. Here any type of flirting is at least unwise. The jealous partner will consider as cheating anything that can indicate even the slightest interest in someone else. If you are jealous of your woman, you will not tolerate her smiles directed at the bartender. It may be completely innocent but the imagination will trick you into thinking all sorts of things and you will end up in a rage. Here we must add that almost certainly the rage is completely unjustified. Jealousy is an unhealthy emotion and triggers unhealthy reactions. What was a simple smile without hinting at anything and not being much of a flirt can be interpreted as an invitation to something sinister. Your overly emotional reaction can lead to unwanted fights or even to an end of the relationship. Such reactions should be avoided at all costs. They are not helping the relationship in any way and can cause a lot of trouble.

Flirting can add lots of fun and even a little spice to a relationship when both partners feel completely secure about their own place in their relationship and about the feelings of their partner. However, when there are any suspicions regarding one of the partners or an unhealthy emotion is involved it can be very devastating. So the question whether flirting is wrong depends entirely on the situation and what exactly the partners themselves feel about it.

How Far to Go Flirting While in a Relationship

When you are in a serious relationship that is important to you then you should keep in mind the emotions and feelings of your woman. You probably have worked out during your time together the kinds of contact outside of your relationship that is ok for both of you. By now you should know if your partner does not mind you having a good time with other women and likewise if you feel fine letting her enjoy the company of other guys. If your partner feels secure about your feelings towards her and is comfortable in a situation when you are flirting with other girls then by all means you can flirt.

There is one thing that you need to remember when you are actually out with your woman, she has to be the center of your attention most of the time, if all of your time is spent flirting with other girls and you fail to give adequate attention to your woman she will feel neglected. Not to mention that it is very rude of you to entirely abandon the company of your own woman and seek that of another's. As long as you make your woman feel that she is the most important to you, it is absolutely fine to smile to and joke with other women. On the other hand, if you concentrate your attention on any one woman noticeably flirting only with her it may seem a bit too much and may stimulate jealous reactions. Your own woman will feel threatened when you allow someone to steal all your attention from her. So make sure that flirting is still fun for your partner and will not get her feelings hurt.

There are situations, however, when you are required to be charming and playful with all the women present. When for instance you are hosting an event of some kind, it will be up to you to help people socialize and mingle, flirting will be a large part of your role. In such a situation your woman should understand your behavior, but it is also your duty to always treat her respectfully, keeping her in your vicinity and making sure that she is also having a good time. If at any time you need to leave her, never leave her alone, you should make sure that there is someone who is going to entertain her while you are gone.

The thing that you should always remember about when you are flirting while in a relationship is that your flirting with other women has to stay light and never become aggressive, and another thing is that you should always refrain from crossing the line of physical contact. Anything even a light touch on the woman's shoulder could be considered as too much in this situation. Even if your woman is tolerant she might get upset witnessing such an action. It is not proper to start serious flirting, it will inevitably mislead the woman you are flirting with as to your intentions and she also may be hurt. Besides, any sinister intent on your part will be frowned upon and may be considered as cheating by your woman. That is even if it will not actually lead you to cheating.

Another thing is when you are flirting out of your woman's sight, when you are out on your own or when you are at work. In this case you will not have to worry that you are under the scrupulous eye of your woman. She will not be jealous obviously not watching your behavior, but that does not mean that you can do whatever you want. Your flirting should always stay within the boundaries of good behavior and acceptable taste. The purpose of flirting will be to enjoy yourself and entertain people around you, and nothing more. Here too, you should not allow yourself to cross the line between fun flirting and serious flirting, keep in mind that you are not seeking a new relationship and you do not want to do anything that would be considered cheating on your partner. That would include serious flirting that involves intimate touching of another woman, even if it will not include any sexual act it will still be well beyond the acceptable action that any partner would allow.

Whenever you are flirting while you are in a relationship you should always stay on the safe side asking yourself if your behavior could hurt someone. If in any doubt better let go, it is always better to miss out on some fun than getting yourself into trouble with people being hurt and relationships being ruined.

Excuses You can Say When You are Caught Flirting with a Girl

A vital thing you need to know about defending yourself against any accusation is that you have to stick to your story, no matter how ridiculous it might be. It will be of no use to change your defense line after some time because then it will be obvious that you are just making up excuses to clean yourself from the guilty actions that you had done, the most central attribute of a liar is consistency. Keeping this in mind, there are a few things you should try to do.

The first strategy is to claim that your girlfriend or whoever is accusing you is simply exaggerating and overreacting. Claim that you were not flirting at all, simply being friendly and funny and that the person must have misinterpreted your actions. As we have mentioned earlier, the line between flirting and being friendly is very thin, and that actually works to your benefit so you should use this as the first line of defense. You must insist that whatever you were doing was just an act of friendliness, that was your one and only intention, and that everything else is just in her head. Some things that might help you out on these are, first of all, explaining to your girlfriend why you would never flirt with that girl. One thing that you could do is criticize the girl in question as much as you can, just make sure that you are out of the girl's earshot when you do that. "Why would I flirt with her when she's not even that pretty?" "She's boring and fat and uses so much make up that she looks like a wax statue, why would I be interested in her?" Remember to always find things that will be believable, you cannot say that she is ugly if she looks like a runway model. After denigrating the girl you were flirting with, what you have to do is convince your girlfriend that she is a lot more interesting and beautiful, so tell her the exact opposite of everything you said about the other girl. "You are so much more interesting and your eyes are so beautiful besides, it is your smile that I want to see first thing in the morning, why would I want someone else in my life?" This should work because you are directly comparing the two girls and showing how one is so much prettier than the other, which is a good thing, on one hand letting your girlfriend knows that she is really special and on the other assuring her that the other girl has nothing that you would be interested in.

Another thing you could say is that you were not the one flirting with the girl, but she was the one who was flirting with you, and you were afraid that if you ignored her you would come as rude and curt. Agree that yes, she was flirting with you, but you were trying to find ways to get out of the situation without being impolite. This argument will be the most reliable as it is so natural for people to want to be esteemed by others and no one wants to ruin their own reputation.

The third thing that you could do is claim that you were not flirting, that it is just the way you behave around people when you are having fun. It has nothing to do with her being a girl, just say that you behave the same way whether you are interacting with a girl or a boy. When you are telling her all that make sure to look her in the eye, it is the way to come through as honest as you can. Of course, if you are not a flirty type of guy in general than this argument will never be believed.

Your last strategy of defense is to simply accuse her back. When she accuses you of flirting with a certain girl just say "What about that guy that was flirting with you all night? You were having a great time and you kept leading him on". Nothing works better than showing someone that he is guilty of the same sin. Show her that you tolerated her flirting with a stranger and in any case for her it was just a fun thing to do so why should not you have the same possibility to enjoy flirting.

The most honest and loyal thing to do, however, is to simply recognize your fault, apologize and promise to try not to do it again. Trying to get out of it, the way we described in previous paragraphs, can be very counterproductive for the relationship since it could lead to the mutual trust being broken. If you really appreciate and care about the girl you are with, the most sensible thing to do is to be honest about your mistake and try to fix it. A good girl is not a frequent thing to come by, so if you have been lucky enough to find one it's a good idea to take good care of her. Honesty, in the long run, pays off.

It is always better to know what is allowed in your relationship and what your girlfriend thinks about flirting in general before you let her witness you smiling at every other beauty you see on your way. As we discussed earlier in the chapter, flirting can actually help a relationship stay fresh and lively, as long as you know how far you can go without upsetting your girlfriend. Let her know how strong your feelings for her are and how much she means to you and you will see that she will not be jealous of your smiles towards other girls.

Tips On How to Add Flirting to a Playful Argument

Even though it should not be overdone or exaggerated, having an argument with your girlfriend or any other girl is actually a great way to have some fun. Being nice and friendly is alright, but there is something exhilarating about confronting your opinions with somebody else, disagreeing, yelling at each other and basically having a pretend-fight.

Engaging in a playful argument can also be a great opportunity to try out things you wouldn't normally do with a girl, such as slapping her in the face (only playing, of course!) or being mean and aggressive. Although there is a line that should never be crossed and it is when you say seriously mean things, if you keep the mood playful and joking, you should be able to say a lot of things that you would have no place to say otherwise.

A fun way to lead an argument is taking extreme point of view that is, exaggerating the thing you want to communicate to the girl in question, in the hopes of eliciting some laughter. Suppose you are angry because she left some dirty dishes in the sink. You could let her know that it bothers you by overreacting and claiming (you should make it clear that you are joking by your facial expressions: a big smile while you say this, not an angry expression) that she always leaves everything dirty in the house and that there is so much garbage in the house you find it difficult to walk around, and there is so much garbage piled up in the driveway you can't get the car out of the garage. These exaggerated claims should make your girl laugh and encourage her to play along, while at the same time letting her know that there is something about her cleaning habits that bothers you.

Also role playing might be a fun thing to try out, again because of the fact that it allows you to try out different standpoints that you normally wouldn't. A fun thing your girl will probably enjoy is you playing the role of her boss who is angry at her for something she did wrong or did not do. You could threaten her with specific consequences unless she amends soon, and she will enjoy trying to find ways to amend and appease your mood. Putting the girl in the victim spot is sure to make her excited. Nothing is as fun as power games, where one actor has the power and the other one has to try to find a way to appease that power. Like a boss/employee situation, and of course she might probably have had sexual fantasies related to her boss, so this is the perfect situation to harmlessly put that into play.

One sure thing to start up a lot of sexual tension is taking the argument into physical ground. This under no circumstance means that you should hit your girl, even as a joke, but rather pretending to fight each other a bit. Girls will especially like being put in the role of the aggressor, where they get to have the power and they are the ones hitting the men, lightly punching them in the ribs or stomach. Then you could switch the roles and have a little struggle as you pretend to assault her while she tries to free herself from your grip. Of course, you could then tackle the girl and throw her on the bed and ravage her and rip off her clothes and do things to her that she would never have even dreamed off.

The most fun part of arguing is the threatening to punish each other if one does not do what other asked them to. "Oh, yeah? Well if you don't clean the room I will tie you to the bed and strip you naked and do unnatural things to you", "Right, so maybe I will not clean the room", "Oh yeah, then, you'll see what I'm capable of doing. Watch this!" Such an argument will escalate and become physical ending up with a hot and wild sex. This all is happening in a fun way, giving you both an exciting and unusual way of releasing tensions and maybe getting to know each other on new grounds.

But no matter what strategy you take, arguing is an activity that involves intense emotions and those emotions should be used to strengthen the relationship, because the strong feelings associated with them are being put to good use.

As you can see flirting can be a life-enhancing game bringing excitement and joy into your life. It is true that for some people it comes easier than for others, but it is a great pastime well worth mastering. If you find it difficult to flirt at the beginning, stay cool and positive, with time all the skills we have introduced will become more natural and you will simply enjoy yourself concentrating on finding the right girls. As your skills improve you can try more challenging options, and with the help of the examples we have provided in this book, you can explore the different scenarios. When you are fully drawn into this exciting game you will come up with your own favorite pick-up lines and original ways to approach strangers. We hope that your new skills will also have impact on your life in general as people will find out that you are a fun person to be around. With a bit of luck your social life will become more satisfying and your friends will envy the ease with which you make contact with the more beautiful part of the population.

Adhering to our principles of healthy and fun flirting will keep you from falling into the pitfalls of the game. There can still be situations where you will need to employ your creativity to get out of, but at least you have the basic tools to protect yourself, and by now you should at least know what situations to avoid and which things are absolutely prohibited in flirting. Be the gentlemen; make it your objective to have fun while at the same time pleasing the woman you are flirting with. What better way to secure yourself success in that playful game?

Finally, if you get attached and find yourself in a relationship, remember that this in no way means that you have to stop flirting altogether. You can and should continue flirting with your partner as that will keep the spark of affection fresh between the two of you. Besides, if you have established your mutual boundaries of conduct and both of you are up for it, then each of you can continue flirting with strangers. As usual moderation is the key here and you have to keep at the back of your head that you need to stay within the limits of dignity and respect for each other's feelings. That way you can safely enjoy the benefits and pleasures of flirting as well as the possibilities that it gives to invigorate you mutual relationship.

We hope that you enjoyed this book on flirting and that this game will bring lots of joy and pleasure into your life.

Made in the USA
Columbia, SC
11 December 2023

28233304R20033